MW00826362

The Not Too Perfect Nativity Play

and Other Dramatic Resources for Christmas

Compiled by Paul M. Miller

Contents

Copyright © 1988 by Lillenas Publishing Company
All rights reserved.   Litho in U.S.A.

Lillenas Publishing Co.
Kansas City, MO 64141

To the Director:

If this is your first time to make use of a collection of Lillenas play scripts, you have discovered what many consider one of the finest sources of dramatic material for the church and Christian school.

Don't stop with your involvement in a Christmas production—go on and discover the possibilities of a broader drama ministry. Secure a copy of the Lillenas Drama and Program Resources Catalog and turn your imagination loose. Also, request to be put on the free subscription list for the quarterly Lillenas Drama Newsletter.

As you direct the material in this collection, remember that each of these scripts has one central goal—to give greater dimension to the age-old story of the Child of Bethlehem.

—PAUL M. MILLER

The Advent Thief

by Neil C. Fitzgerald

Cast of Characters:
> MOM
> TAD: *Son, age 5*
> JEFF: *Son, age 15*
> MELISSA: *Daughter, age 11*
> AUNT KATE: *A woman in her 70's*
> NANCY: *A girl, age 12*
> POLICEMAN
> BOY: *Age 10*
> DAD

Setting:
The scene is a combination living/dining room. To stage left is a couch flanked by easy chairs and other furniture. On stage right is a dining room table and chairs set for five. An unlit Advent wreath is on the table. To the left is a door to the outside. Next to it is a closet door. On the right is a doorway that leads to the rest of the house.

Costumes:
All characters wear contemporary clothes.

Props:
Two purses, checkbook, pen, money, card box, Advent wreath, table settings, children's book, magazine, paper bag, bowl, and matches.

(As play begins MOM *is seated on the sofa thumbing through a magazine.* TAD *enters from the right carrying a book.)*

TAD *(climbing onto the sofa):* Mommy, will you read to me? *(Hands* MOM *the book.)*

MOM *(putting the magazine aside and taking the book):* Well, Tad, only for a short while. Your father will be home soon, and I have things in the oven.

TAD *(points to a page):* Read there.

MOM *(reading):* "Caesar Augustus published a decree ordering a census."

TAD: Mommy, who was Caesar Augustus?

MOM: He was the ruler in Judea during the days when Jesus was born.

TAD: Like our president?

MOM: Somewhat.

TAD: Only he wasn't as nice.

MOM: You might put it that way.

TAD: What's a census?

MOM: That's when all the people have to be counted. Joseph had to go to Bethlehem to be counted, because that was where he and his ancestors were from.

TAD: And he took Mary with him.

MOM: That's right.

TAD: And Mary rode a donkey.

MOM: Yes.

TAD: I just know that I'm going to get a donkey for Christmas. That's all I want, a donkey.

MOM: Tad, I haven't seen any donkeys at Macy's Department Store. I do know they have many wonderful kittens and puppies.

TAD: Mommy, Baby Jesus had a donkey, and that's what I want.

MOM *(hearing arguing from another room):* Jeff! Melissa! Come in here right now! (JEFF *and* MELISSA *run into the living room.)*

MELISSA: It just isn't fair!

JEFF: Listen to who's talking about being fair!

MOM: Hold it, both of you. Let's discuss this calmly. Jeff, you first.

JEFF: I had the football game on, and Melissa just walked up to the set and switched the channel.

MELISSA: I get to watch what I want on Saturdays.

JEFF: That wasn't our agreement.

MOM: Just what was your agreement? I thought this was all settled at the beginning of the football season.

JEFF: When pro football is on, I get to watch.

MELISSA: On Sunday!

MOM: Wait a minute. You two have lost me. This is Saturday.

JEFF: But, Mom, when the college season ends, they play pro ball on Saturday. And this is a big game.

MOM: I suppose there's another game on tomorrow.

MELISSA: A doubleheader, Mom. How much football can a person take?

JEFF: But this is crunch time. Everything is up for grabs.

MOM: Your father should be home any minute. I think we need his counsel.

JEFF: Mom, now you know why I want Melissa to have her own portable TV for Christmas. I told you and Dad I'm willing to sacrifice, to go without any presents just so Melissa can have her own TV.

MOM: Sacrifice? Jeff, your spirit of giving is a bit tarnished. For now turn the TV off. I presume you both can find some homework that needs to be done before Monday morning.

TAD *(bored with the conversation; goes to the front of the stage and peers toward the audience):* Mommy, Aunt Kate is coming.

MOM: Oh, that's right. She said she was dropping by with some presents.

MELISSA: Why does she bring them by so early?

MOM: She's afraid something might happen, and she won't get them to us.

JEFF: Yeah, every Christmas she says it will probably be her last Christmas.

MELISSA: She doesn't look sick to me.

MOM: She isn't. Her mother lived to be nearly a hundred, and I think Aunt Kate might outdo her.

TAD: I don't see any packages.

JEFF: You won't, Tad. Aunt Kate's presents are always microscopic.

MELISSA: Let's face it. Aunt Kate is a Scrooge.

MOM: Enough you two.

TAD: What is a Scrooge?

JEFF: A person with a lot of money who won't spend it.

MELISSA: Last year Aunt Kate gave me a matchbox with a poem inside.

MOM: The poem was beautiful, and I know she spent some time decorating the matchbox.

TAD: What did she give you, Jeff?

JEFF: A picture of Great-Grandfather.

MOM: It wasn't easy for her to part with that picture, Jeff.

JEFF: I suppose not.

(Doorbell rings. The children all leave.)

MOM *(opening outside door):* Aunt Kate, come in. It's so good to see you.

AUNT KATE *(enters):* I can't stay, mind you. I just came by to leave these gifts for the children. *(Hands MOM a small paper bag.)*

MOM: Do sit down for a minute.

AUNT KATE: Well, only for a minute.

(AUNT KATE sits on the sofa. MOM sits on an easy chair.)

MOM: Well, tell me, how have you been?

AUNT KATE: Surviving, barely. Expect this will be my last Christmas. How are the children?

MOM: Oh, they're fine.

AUNT KATE: Jeff still wearing that long hair?

MOM: Yes.

AUNT KATE: If he were mine, I'd sneak into his room each night and snip off a bit of hair. It would be short again in no time. He'd never know what happened.

MOM: It might work. Jeff can be oblivious to things at times.

AUNT KATE: I suppose Melissa wants to wear makeup.

MOM: She is growing up.

AUNT KATE: I wasn't allowed to wear makeup until I got a job and began to support myself. Even then I didn't bother. It's a waste of money, you know. TV is always trying to get us to waste our money. I can hardly bear to watch it. And Tad, how is the darling? I imagine he can't wait for Christmas to come.

MOM: Well, he's given us a real dilemma this year.

AUNT KATE: Oh?

MOM: He wants a donkey for Christmas.

AUNT KATE: No problem. I saw some stuffed donkeys in a store just the other day. Now where was that?

MOM: Oh, that it was that simple. Tad has made it quite clear. He wants a *real* donkey.

AUNT KATE *(surprised):* A live donkey! For heaven's sake, why?

MOM: Because that's what Baby Jesus had.

AUNT KATE: What an adorable thought! So what are you going to do?

MOM: I don't know. We thought maybe we could convince him a kitten or a puppy would be nice, but no, he insists that he is going to get a donkey.

AUNT KATE *(laughing):* I'll be interested to learn how you make out.

(Doorbell rings.)

MOM *(calling):* Melissa, will you get the door?

MELISSA *(running through the room to the door):* Hi, Aunt Kate. *(Opening the door, greets* NANCY*)* Oh, hi, Nancy.

NANCY: Melissa, I'm selling Christmas cards. Would you like to buy some? They're five dollars a box.

MELISSA: Mom?

MOM: Well, your father and I have all the cards we need. Maybe, though, you and Jeff could split a box.

MELISSA: OK.

MOM *(reaching below end table for her purse,* MOM *hands* MELISSA *a five dollar bill):* Here's the money.

MELISSA: How about you, Aunt Kate?

AUNT KATE: Oh, heavens no. I stopped sending Christmas cards when the price of a stamp went to five cents. I see no reason why we should subsidize the post office.

MELISSA *(handing* NANCY *the money):* Here, Nancy.

NANCY *(handing* MELISSA *the box of cards):* Thanks.

MELISSA: Bye, Nancy. I'll see you in school tomorrow.

NANCY: Bye, everyone.

*(*NANCY *exits.* MELISSA *closes the door.)*

MELISSA *(starting across the room):* Well, back to the homework.

AUNT KATE: Come over here a moment, Melissa. *(*MELISSA *walks slowly over to* AUNT KATE *who stares at her face.)* Good.

MELISSA: What's good?

AUNT KATE: Your lips.

MELISSA *(perplexed):* May I please go now?

AUNT KATE: Of course.

(MELISSA *exits right.*)

AUNT KATE *(rising):* Well, I must be leaving.

MOM: Wouldn't you like to stay for dinner? We have plenty.

AUNT KATE: No, I appreciate the invitation, but I want to do some errands before the stores close.

MOM: Well, the invitation is still open if you change your mind. *(She walks* AUNT KATE *to the door.)* Thanks again for the presents.

AUNT KATE: I hope the children like them.

MOM: I'm sure they'll be as surprised as last year. Bye, Aunt Kate.

AUNT KATE: Bye. *(Exits.)*

TAD *(running into the room carrying his book):* Mommy, now can you read to me?

MOM: Oh, Tad, I should prepare the dinner.

TAD: Please, Mommy, just for a few minutes.

MOM: All right, but only for five minutes.

(MOM *sits on the sofa.* TAD *climbs up beside her and hands her the book.* MOM *opens the book and starts reading.)*

MOM: "Caesar Augustus published a decree ordering . . ."

(A loud commotion outside the door interrupts them. AUNT KATE, *distraught, rushes into the room and starts screaming.* JEFF *and* MELISSA *come running.)*

AUNT KATE *(yelling):* Help! Call the police! I've been robbed! A boy just grabbed my purse and ran down the street!

JEFF: I'll call the police. *(Exits.)*

MOM: Aunt Kate, sit down and tell us what happened.

AUNT KATE *(sitting):* I'm just so upset.

MOM: I'm sure you are, but try to stay calm.

AUNT KATE: It all happened so fast. I just got to the bottom of your steps and walked half way down the block. I didn't even see him until he ripped the purse from my hand. He nearly knocked me down.

MOM: Well, we're all thankful you weren't hurt.

JEFF *(entering):* The police said they have a car in the neighborhood. Maybe they can catch him.

AUNT KATE: They've got to catch him.

MELISSA: Did you get a good look at him, Aunt Kate?

AUNT KATE: Oh, I'd know him again. People like that shouldn't be allowed on the street.

JEFF: Did you have a lot of money in your purse, Aunt Kate?

AUNT KATE: No, but there is my checkbook and house key and other personal things. *(Visibly upset.)* Oh, I just don't know what I'm going to do.

TAD: Don't cry, Aunt Kate. Daddy will be home soon, and he always knows what to do.

(Doorbell rings. JEFF *opens the door to a* POLICEMAN *holding a purse in one hand and a* BOY *in the other.)*

JEFF: Boy, that was fast.

AUNT KATE *(rushes to the* POLICEMAN *and takes the purse):* Oh, you found my purse. Thank you. Thank you. Thank you.

POLICEMAN: Actually I spotted the boy running down the street just as the call came in.

AUNT KATE: That's the boy all right. Why you wretched child. Why did you do that to me?

BOY: Because you looked rich, and we didn't have any money and it's almost Christmas.

AUNT KATE: So you thought you'd steal from some helpless woman and buy out the toy store.

BOY *(protesting):* No, I stole so we could eat.

POLICEMAN: I know the boy, Ma'am. He is one of the Jenkins family. His mother recently lost her job, and she's trying to bring up four boys all by herself.

AUNT KATE *(flustered):* Well . . . still . . . that's no reason to steal.

POLICEMAN: Then you want me to take him down to the station, Ma'am?

AUNT KATE: Of course I do. He has to learn just like the rest of us.

POLICEMAN: Then we'll be on our way.

*(*POLICEMAN *and* BOY *exit.)*

TAD *(after a pause):* Is it too late to write another letter to Santa Claus, Mommy?

MOM: I suppose not, but why do you want to write to Santa Claus again?

TAD: To tell him not to bring me a donkey. I want him to bring some food to that boy's family instead. No one should be hungry at Christmas.

AUNT KATE *(after a pause):* Oh, I don't know what gets into me some times. Jeff, hurry and stop them.

JEFF: I'll catch them. *(Exits.)*

AUNT KATE *(fumbling in her purse):* I've got to clean this purse out one of these days. *(Removes checkbook and pen and follows JEFF.)*

MELISSA: Aunt Kate is acting weird, Mom. What's happened to her?

MOM: I think she's had a visit from Jacob Marley.

TAD: Who is Jacob Marley, Mommy?

MOM: Just a friend from an old Christmas story. I'll tell you all about him when I have more time.

MELISSA: Yeah, he's scary but he's someone to listen to. We read all about him in school this week.

JEFF *(entering):* Boy, I knew Aunt Kate was rich but . . . Mom, you should see the check she is writing.

MOM: What Aunt Kate is doing I don't think she would want us to discuss with anyone.

JEFF: Right, Mom. I understand.

MELISSA: I'm hungry.

MOM: Dinner will be ready soon.

AUNT KATE *(entering):* Did someone mention dinner? I hope that invitation is still open. *(Puts checkbook and pen back into purse.)*

MOM: It certainly is. Jeff, take Aunt Kate's coat.

(JEFF *takes the coat and hangs it in the closet.)*

MOM: Melissa, you set another place, and, Jeff, bring another chair from your room. (JEFF *and* MELISSA *exit.)*

AUNT KATE *(taking* TAD *by the hand):* Now, young man, perhaps you can show me where to wash up.

TAD: Oh, I can.

AUNT KATE: By the way, Tad, you won't have to send Santa Claus that other letter. I assure you the Jenkins family will have plenty to eat this Christmas. And you remember that little Jenkins boy?

TAD: Yes.

AUNT KATE: Well, I made him promise never to steal again and to come and see me whenever he has a problem. And speaking of problems, Tad, it seems you have a mighty big one.

TAD: I do?

AUNT KATE: Yes, you do. When you receive your donkey, where are you going to put it?

TAD *(perplexed):* In my room?

AUNT KATE: I don't think that's such a good idea. But you know I have a very big yard and an old shed just standing empty. (AUNT KATE *and* TAD *exit.)*

DAD *(entering):* Hello, honey. *(Hanging his coat in the closet.)* How was your day?

MOM: Interesting to say the least.

DAD: Oh?

MOM: For one thing I do believe that there is going to be a certain donkey under the Christmas tree this year.

DAD: You're kidding. *(Pause.)* Tell me you're kidding.

MOM: It's really going to happen. I'll tell you all about it later. Aunt Kate is here. She is going to have dinner with us.

DAD: But she never accepts dinner invitations.

MOM: Neither did Mr. Scrooge until . . .

(AUNT KATE, TAD, JEFF, *and* MELISSA *return.* MELISSA *puts dishes and silverware on the table.* JEFF *holds chair for* AUNT KATE. Mom *exits.)*

DAD: Aunt Kate, it's a joy to have you with us.

AUNT KATE *(sitting):* It's nice to be with the family.

TAD: Daddy, can I sit next to Aunt Kate?

DAD: Yes, you may. *(All sit.)*

MOM *(returns and sets a large bowl onto the table):* I'm afraid it's only stew, Aunt Kate. *(Sits.)*

AUNT KATE: But I love stew. *(Pause.)* Well, we know what Tad wants for Christmas. How about the rest of you?

JEFF: I know Melissa wants a portable . . . *(Pause.)* I guess just being together is the best gift of all.

MOM: Dad, would you say the Advent prayer, and, Aunt Kate, will you do the honor and light the first candle. *(Hands* AUNT KATE *the matches.)*

AUNT KATE: Thank you.

DAD: Let us pray. O God, by whose word all things are sanctified, pour forth thy blessing upon this wreath, and grant that we who use it may prepare our hearts for the coming of Christ and may receive from thee abundant graces.

ALL: Amen.

(AUNT KATE *lights one of the four candles in the wreath. Blackout.*)

The Not Too Perfect Nativity Play

by Bonnie Zimmer

Acknowledgment
My sincere thanks to Bob MacKenzie and Barbara Kehrstephan for
their advice, encouragement, and laughter!

—BONNIE

Here is a play that may stretch your production capabilities, but the effort will
be well worth it. Of unusual interest will be the use of children, teens, and
adults. This is an all-church play in the truest sense.

The Cast:

Adults:

MISS TATE: *the youth group leader; a teacher by profession. She is enthusiastic
and confident.*

MRS. BAXTER: *Ian's mother. She is a pleasant lady. She is 6-7 months pregnant.
She has the role of Mary in the Nativity Play.*

MRS. WALTERS: *mother of Kimmie and Darcy. She has a lot of confidence and
tends to be outspoken. She has the role of the Head Angel.*

MR. THOMAS: *father of Cindy, Karen, and Bobby. He is a pleasant, easy-going
man. He speaks slowly with just a hint of a drawl. He has the role of Shepherd No. 3 in the play.*

MRS. THOMAS: *his wife. She is a pleasant, motherly type. She is an angel in the
play.*

MR. CALDER: *father of Duncan and Paul. He is a self-confident businessman. He
has the role of Shepherd No. 1*

MRS. CALDER: *his wife. She is an angel in the play.*

MR. HARPER: *Father of the twins (Jim and Jan). He is a small, thin man who
appears nervous and fidgety. He plays the role of Joseph.*

MR. GREY: *father of Sandra and Tara. He plays the role of the innkeeper.*

MRS. GREY: *his wife. She is an angel in the play.*

Teenagers: *(All are in the 14-16 range.)*

CINDY: *has a cheery, positive manner. She is an angel in the play.*

MARJ: *tends to be pessimistic; an angel in the play.*

TRISHA: *has recently moved to town, is not as sure of herself as the others; angel.*

SUSAN: *pleasant, excitable, an angel.*

TARA: *very self-confident, a leader, angel.*

CATHY: *Paul's girlfriend, aggressive, quick-tempered; Narrator No. 1 in the play.*

ANNE: *not easily excited, has a dry sense of humor; has role of the innkeeper's granddaughter.*

JAN: *stubborn, not easily intimidated; Narrator No. 2 in the play.*

IAN: *Paul's side-kick, easy-going. He is a Wise Man.*

PAUL: *very self-confident, sees himself as being very "cool." He is Shepherd No. 4 in the play.*

DARCY: *he has recently moved to town and is quite impressed by* TIM. *He is a Wise Man.*

TIM: *sure of himself, takes his pet flea very seriously and expects others to do so, too. He is a Wise Man as well.*

JIM: *Jan's twin, just as stubborn as she is; Shepherd No. 2 in the play.*

(*Note:* If one of the female teenagers is a capable pianist, she could be the pianist for the play, rather than being an angel in the choir.)

Children:

KIMMIE WALTERS: *a spoiled, bratty eight-year-old. She is a sheep in the play.*

KAREN THOMAS: *a five-year-old. She is an angel in the play.*

BOBBY THOMAS: *her six-year-old brother. He is a calf in the play.*

DUNCAN CALDER: *an eight-year-old, loud and boisterous. He is a donkey in the play.*

SANDRA GREY: *seven years old, rather shy. She is a sheep in the play.*

Playing Time:

Approximately 70 minutes.

Production Notes:

Stage Design and Sets: All the action takes place on the stage area of a church auditorium. An aisle down through the audience will be used as one of the entrances. Stage entrances are stage right and upstage left.

Stage setup for rehearsal scene: Fourteen or 15 chairs are placed downstage left, slightly at an angle to improve visibility. These will be used by the parents and children for the meeting scene. There is a small table downstage right, where scripts are piled. A set of risers should be placed upstage right, on an angle. These will be used by the youth group. Upstage and slightly to the left is a large table that will be used for costume boxes.

Stage setup for the Nativity Play: Risers will be upstage during the entire play. In the opening scene (Joseph and Mary's arrival at the inn), there is a small, rough table downstage left, and a chair. The shepherds' scene could be presented in a spotlight in the downstage left area, and the manger scene could be placed in the downstage right area of the stage.

(*Note:* Accompanying diagrams will help clarify suggested locations of sets.)

Lighting: Stage area is fully lit for the rehearsal scene. Spotlights may be used for scenes in the Nativity Play. Soft lighting may be used on the Angel choir when they sing between scenes.

Makeup: Everyone should look "natural" in the rehearsal scene. Some "aging" of characters will be necessary in the Nativity Play. (MR. GREY and WISE MEN)

Costumes: For the rehearsal scene, everyone is dressed in everyday clothes. The young people should dress as they do for school. MR. CALDER may wear a business suit; MR. HARPER and MR. GREY could wear sweaters and dress slacks; and MR. THOMAS's clothes should look slightly Western. Slacks and blouses or sweaters would be suitable for the mothers. MISS TATE should be dressed in a skirt and blouse or a full-skirted dress. Perhaps she could be a little fussy. All actors entering from the floor of the auditorium should wear coats, or be carrying them, as it is assumed that they have come into the auditorium from outside. MR. HARPER and MRS. WALTERS may wear glasses.

In the Nativity Play, people will be wearing traditional biblical costumes. It will be helpful to have animal costumes (sheep, donkey, calf) or masks for children.

Props: Students should carry books, purses, gym bags, etc., when they first enter, as it is assumed that they are coming from school to the rehearsal. Other props: scripts and stapler, boxes of costumes, halos, crowns, small box for the flea, miniature butterfly net, shepherds' crooks, Wise Men's gifts, bundles of wood, twigs, handfuls of dried grasses, manger, straw, doll, small stool for Mary, cane and bag of coins for the innkeeper.

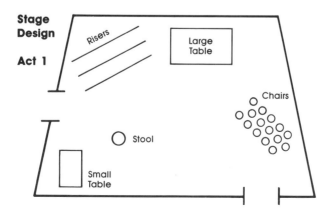

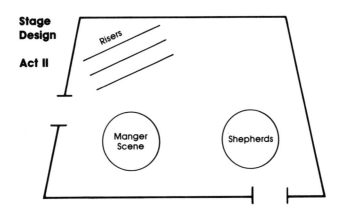

Stage Design

Act II

Risers

Manger Scene

Shepherds

Note: If built-in stage curtains are not available, you may wish to stretch a wire across the playing area and hang fabric from drapery hooks. Or you could construct two formers from 1″ x 2″ lumber, covered with fabric. These may be pushed or pulled to simulate stage curtains. It is also possible to do away with the need for such curtains altogether.

Act I

Setting: The stage area of a church auditorium.

Time: The present, a few weeks before Christmas.

(As the play begins, CINDY *is alone on center stage, looking out toward the audience, doing facial flexibility exercises: opens mouth wide, purses lips, lets tongue swing from side to side, etc. After a few seconds she switches to articulation exercises.)*

CINDY: Loo, loo, loo, loo. Law, law, law, law. Lay, lay, lay, lay. Lee, lee, lee, lee. "The tip of the tongue, the lips, the teeth."

MARJ *(entering from upstage right):* What are you doing, Cindy?

CINDY: I'm warming up for the rehearsal. "The tip of the tongue, the lips, the teeth . . ."

MARJ: You're wasting your time, you know. I don't think our parts in the play are going to be very big this year. I hear that most of our work is going to be backstage.

CINDY *(doing physical warmups):* What do you think of Miss Tate's plan?

MARJ: I think it'll be a disaster. Once you get a bunch of novices involved in a theatrical production, you're asking for trouble. I don't know why our youth group couldn't just produce the play on its own, like it always has.

CINDY: I'm kind of nervous about it, too. Did you tell your parents about the plan?

MARJ: Are you kidding? I had no intention of being alone in the house with them when the yelling started.

CINDY: Me neither. I just told mine about the meeting, that's all.

(The lights suddenly go off, leaving stage and audience in total darkness.)

MARJ: Hey! What happened to the lights?

CINDY: Maybe the power is off.

PAUL *(in a ghost-like voice from the back of the auditorium):* Helloooooo, my friends . . .

MARJ: Oh, it's not a power failure, that's Paul's voice. Paul, you turn those lights on right now!

IAN *(in a hollow voice):* They appear to be very frightened indeed.

MARJ: I recognize your voice too, Ian. Now just end your little joke and turn the lights back on.

PAUL: Their fear is building to a higher and more intensive pitch. At any moment now they will be screaming in terror!

MARJ: OK, you two. I give up. I'll scream for you. *(Yelling.)* TURN THE LIGHTS BACK ON!

IAN: Ow, my eardrums. You guys are no fun at all.

CINDY *(as all the houselights and stage lights come on):* We don't need *all* the lights. Miss Tate said she was going to hold the meeting on the stage.

(Houselights are turned off and just stage lights are left on.)

PAUL *(approaching stage):* So what important discussion did we interrupt?

MARJ: We were talking about Miss Tate's plan for the Nativity Play. What do you two think of her idea?

IAN *(as he grabs a chair):* Ask Paul. You know I don't think after school hours.

PAUL: Just a minute. *(Strikes the classical thinker's pose, begins to make odd noises, grimaces.)*

CINDY: Is he going to be sick?

IAN: Shh . . . He's concentrating.

PAUL: After great deliberation I would conclude the play will either be a huge success or a huge failure. That'll be 50 cents please.

MARJ *(shaking her head):* Can't you guys *ever* be serious?

(PAUL *attempts to pull down corners of his mouth with his fingers, then shrugs and puts his feet up on a chair, his back to the upstage entrance.*)

(TRISHA, SUSAN, TARA, *and* ANNE *enter from upstage right.* TARA *and* ANNE *are carrying boxes of costumes.*)

ANNE: Hi, everybody. Has Miss Tate come in yet?

(ANNE *and* TARA *go to large table upstage left, where they place boxes and then begin to look through them.*)

MARJ: No, we haven't seen her. Where are Darcy and Tim?

SUSAN: I'm not sure *they'll* get here at all. Tim is busy chasing that flea he is so fond of.

MARJ *(groaning):* Oh, when is he going to grow up? Who ever heard of a 15-year-old with a pet flea?

TRISHA: Yeah, I wonder why he'd want a flea?

TARA: Well, I guess it wasn't his first choice. His sister told me that when he was nine years old, he wanted a puppy really badly, but his parents wouldn't let him have one. So he decided that if he couldn't have the pup, then at least he'd have the flea, and he's had one ever since.

TRISHA: The same one? I didn't know fleas lived that long.

TARA: No, he's had four fleas since then. This one is actually Freddie the Fifth.

TRISHA: What happened to the others?

TARA *(counting them off on her fingers):* Freddie the First was hit by a Tonka truck. Freddie the Second was swallowed by a cat. And Freddies Third and Fourth died of natural causes.

TRISHA: Boy, that's sure a strange pet. A fellow at Riverton High had a pet boa once, but I think this is worse. This flea business makes me itch all the time.

PAUL: Girls, please! As a good friend of Tim and his flea, I can't sit here and just listen to all this. Freddie is absolutely harmless and has proved to be a loyal pal. Personally, I think having a flea is even better than having a girlfriend.

(CATHY *has appeared at back, carrying some halos and crowns. She stands listening, growing visibly angrier as* PAUL *talks.*)

PAUL *(continuing):* Just think of the money a guy could save—no pizzas to share or milkshakes to buy. And if you got tired of the flea hanging around, you could just pop it into a little box and put it into your pocket. Simple.

CATHY *(walks over behind him and shoves a halo down over his head so that half his face is covered):* Of all the nerve! A little box! Somebody's going to need a box for *you* right away—a big one!

PAUL: Oh, hi, Cath! You're here! Ha ha . . . I didn't see you come in.

CATHY: Obviously not! *(Turns and stomps back to the costume table.)*

PAUL *(trailing behind her and trying to remove halo):* You know, Cath . . . you don't eat much pizza . . . usually . . . uh, I was just referring to girlfriends *in general,* not you in particular . . . *(Sighs.)* Oh, well.

CATHY: Spare me the apologies until you have rehearsed a bit—improvisation has never been your strong point. *(To the others.)* Where's Miss Tate? I have a message for her.

SUSAN: She should be here any minute now . . . I thought I just heard someone in the hall. *(Glances off right)* Maybe that's her. Oh . . . no I guess not.

(TIM and DARCY enter, stage right. TIM is talking to something on his elbow.)

TIM: Look, if you're going to be like that, I'll take you home right now!

DARCY: What does he want, Tim?

TIM: He wants a part in the Christmas play—a big part.

ANNE *(dryly):* Well he'll have to do some work on voice projection then.

SUSAN *(wrinkles her nose):* Tim, why don't you put that flea away for a while. The parents are going to start arriving any minute.

TIM *(looking puzzled):* Freddie? Freddie? Freddie, where are you? Oh . . .

TRISHA: What's the matter?

TIM: He's gone. You girls must have hurt his feelings. You know how sensitive he is. Everybody help me look. Here, Freddie!

(TIM takes out a miniature butterfly net to begin the chase. Others begin to move around the stage, looking as well. TRISHA stands back from the action, unwilling to get too close to the flea.)

ANNE: I can't believe we do these crazy things.

PAUL: Oh, come on, you know life would be pretty dull without Freddie— especially geography class. Here, Freddie, Freddie, Freddie . . .

TIM: Don't anybody step on him!

IAN: Hey, that's right. That would make him "Freddie the Flat Flea," wouldn't it?

TIM: I've spotted him moving. Stand still, Tara. I'll just reach around like this . . . *(Puts arm around TARA and looks pleased with himself.)*

TARA *(threateningly):* Watch it, Tim.

TIM *(releasing her):* Now you scared him away. There he goes . . .

(TIM *follows movements with his head—flea is obviously hopping, and lands on* CINDY's *shoe.)*

TIM: Don't move your foot, Cindy. (TIM *gets down on all fours and is just about to capture the flea when it jumps once more.)* That was a good flip, Freddie . . . now just do one more . . . good boy!

(TIM *quickly places butterfly net over Freddie and pops him into his box.)*

TIM: There you go!

TRISHA *(apprehensively):* Are you sure he's in there?

TIM *(grinning):* Of course! Wanna see? *(Moves to open box right under her nose.)*

TRISHA *(quickly):* No thanks!

(MISS TATE *enters from stage right.)*

ANNE: Hi, Miss Tate. We found those boxes that you had been asking about.

MISS TATE: Oh, that's good. Have you looked in them yet?

ANNE: Yes, and I think all the costumes are there, but some of them are mixed up.

MISS TATE: Why don't you and some of the other girls do the sorting right now, and fellows, you can look backstage for the props. Oh, and I need two people to staple the scripts that are on the small table over there.

(IAN *and* SUSAN *raise hands to indicate they will do this.* CATHY *goes over to speak to* MISS TATE *while others begin the jobs they have been asked to do. The costume sorting is done right at the large table.* MRS. WALTERS *and* KIMMIE *enter from back of the auditorium.)*

MISS TATE *(calling from the stage):* Hello, Mrs. Walters. Hi, Kimmie.

MRS. WALTERS: Hello, Miss Tate.

MISS TATE: You can leave your coats on the chairs down front. *(Indicates a row of chairs at front of audience.)* We'll be holding the meeting up here.

MRS. WALTERS *(as she removes coat and helps* KIMMIE): Here, let me help you, Kimmie.

KIMMIE *(whining):* Mom, you're pulling my hair.

(DARCY *appears at stage left, carrying shepherds' crooks.* MRS. WALTERS *calls out in a sing-song voice as she spots him.)*

MRS. WALTERS: Hello, Darcy! Look, Kimmie, there's big brother!

DARCY: Hi, Mom. What's *she* doing here? *(Points at* KIMMIE.)

MISS TATE: I phoned and told her to bring Kimmie, too, Darcy. *(She takes crooks from him and takes them over to the costume table.)*

DARCY *(without enthusiasm):* Oh, great. (KIMMIE *makes a horrible face at him.)* Watch it, pipsqueak!

MRS. WALTERS: Darcy, you must quit calling little Kimmie those names.

DARCY: But, Mom, if you could just *see* some of those faces she makes sometimes.

MRS. WALTERS: Let me see your face, Kimmie, dear. (KIMMIE *smiles sweetly.)* That's nice. Smile at your brother, dear. (KIMMIE *exaggerates the smile until it is a grimace.)* And who is this, Darcy? *(She points to* TIM *who has just come up behind* DARCY. *He is carrying the Wise Men's gifts.)* Don't forget your manners!

DARCY: This is Tim O'Kell, Mom. Tim, this is my mother.

MRS. WALTERS *(enthusiastically):* I'm pleased to meet you, Tim. I'm glad Darcy has already made some friends—some *neatly dressed* friends. *(To* DARCY*)* Some of the boys you chummed with in Beckridge were so grubby that I was afraid to let them in the house. *(Shivers)* Ugh.

DARCY: They were a lot of fun, Mom.

MRS. WALTERS *(frowning):* Hmmm. *(More brightly.)* All the same, I am sure I'm going to like Tim better. *(To* TIM*)* You'll have to come to the house some time to meet Mr. Walters. Come along, Kimmie, let's sit down.

(THOMASES, GREYS, CALDERS, *and* MRS. BAXTER *enter from back of the auditorium.* MISS TATE *moves to front of stage to greet them.)*

MISS TATE: Here are some more parents. Hello, everyone! You can leave your coats down there and then come on up and take a seat. Susan, have you done a head count of the youth group members?

SUSAN: Yes, Miss Tate. Everyone's here except the twins. They were going to come with their father 'cause they had a driving lesson today.

MISS TATE: OK, we'll wait a few minutes, then. Oh, hello, Mrs. Baxter *(as* MRS. BAXTER *comes up the steps),* I hear you do a lot of sewing ... there's something over here I'd like to get your opinion on. *(They move back to the costume table.)*

(During MRS. BAXTER's *conversation with* MISS TATE, IAN *pretends to be engrossed in his stapling.* SUSAN *looks sideways at him a couple of times and then finally gives him a poke.)*

SUSAN: Ian!

IAN: Huh? *(Looks up.)*

SUSAN *(incredulously):* Ian, isn't that your mother?

(IAN *looks over as though he is straining to see.)*

IAN *(slowly):* Yeah, that looks like her all right.

SUSAN: You didn't tell us she was *pregnant!*

IAN: I was hoping nobody'd notice.

SUSAN: Aren't you excited about it?

IAN: Yeah, well, not exactly. It's a little embarrassing. I thought parents were supposed to know better.

SUSAN: Aren't you looking forward to having a little brother or sister?

IAN: Oh, yes, I'm just thrilled. While all my pals are out driving fast cars and chasing girls, I'm going to be stuck at home changing wet diapers—yech!

SUSAN: Oh cheer up, it won't be that bad. I'm sure your mom will get sitters. I'd be willing to baby-sit—I love babies. Come on, I'm going to offer my services right now. *(She drags IAN over with her as the HARPERS come in.)*

(HARPERS enter from back of the auditorium. The twins are in the midst of a heated debate.)

JAN: I did not!

JIM: You did so! You went right on past the stop sign. I'll bet you didn't even see it.

JAN: Of course I saw it!

JIM: Well, why didn't you stop?

JAN: Because I couldn't see anything from there.

JIM: Don't you know that you're supposed to stop at the stop sign and then inch forward?

JAN: I stopped when I could see what was coming!

JIM: Yeah, smack in the middle of the intersection—good thing we weren't all killed!

JAN: Well, at least I didn't bounce off the curb when I did my parallel parking. It'd be a miracle if Mr. Barrow doesn't sue for whiplash.

MR. HARPER *(words spaced evenly and slowly as if he is trying to control himself):* If you two don't quit your bickering, I will not ride *anywhere* with *either* of you for a month. Understood?

(The twins glare at one another. They go to sit on opposite ends of the risers when MISS TATE asks people to sit down.)

MISS TATE: If everyone will sit down now, I think we could begin the meeting . . .

(Adults sit on chairs, downstage left, young people on risers, except TARA, PAUL, and ANNE, who sit or lean on costume table. MISS TATE should stand or sit on a high stool downstage right.)

MISS TATE: I'm really pleased to see so many parents and children here this afternoon. As you know, we begin rehearsals today for our annual Nativity Play. It's going to be similar to what has been done in the past, with one major difference, and that's where you parents come in. *(Slight pause during which a few parents look at one another, puzzled and a bit apprehensive.)* This year, we thought we'd add some special interest to the play by giving all the lead roles to parents. *(Enthusiastically.)* So what do you think?

(There is momentary silence.)

MRS. CALDER *(shaking her head in disbelief):* You're not serious!

MRS. THOMAS: Do you mean we'll be *acting?*

MISS TATE: That's right. It would make the play very realistic. Some of the young people will have minor roles too, and the others will be working backstage.

MRS. CALDER: But Miss Tate, the youth group has *always* acted in the Christmas Play. What will people think if we take the parts?

MISS TATE: They'll love it! In communities of this size, most people know one another, right? *(Parents nod.)* Well, they'll be very eager to watch their friends and neighbors on stage, you'll see. If you agree to act, I'm sure we can count on a *very* large audience.

(Groans and exclamations of nervous excitement from the parents. Youth group members glance at one another.)

MRS. GREY: I know I'll just die if I have to talk in front of a lot of people.

TARA: That's OK, Mom. We'll just improvise a funeral scene.

MISS TATE: We can give you a non-speaking part if you'd prefer, Mrs. Grey.

MRS. BAXTER: Well, I think it's a great idea, Miss Tate, but there's no way I can go on stage looking like this.

IAN: That's for sure!

SUSAN: Ian!

MISS TATE: Mrs. Baxter, I think I have the *perfect* part for you!

MRS. BAXTER *(understanding):* Of course!

MRS. THOMAS: I'd love to try to act. I'm just not sure that my nerves can take it.

CINDY *(embarrassed):* Oh, Mom!

MRS. BAXTER *(to MRS. THOMAS):* Stella, if my nerves can stand it, yours certainly can!

MISS TATE: Perhaps you could have a non-speaking part as well, Mrs. Thomas.

MRS. WALTERS *(waving her hand):* Miss Tate! I don't mind at all taking a speaking part. I enjoy being "in the spotlight" so to speak.

MISS TATE: Oh . . . good . . . now . . . how about some of the men—how do you feel about acting?

MR. CALDER: I think it would be an interesting experience—I'd be willing to try.

MR. GREY: As long as there aren't too many lines to learn, I'll take a part.

MISS TATE: OK . . . how about you, Mr. Thomas?

MR. THOMAS: Well, I'm probably better at ropin' steers than I am at actin', Miss Tate, but I'm always game for some fun. I'll give it a try.

MISS TATE: Wonderful. Mr. Harper?

MR. HARPER *(nervously):* Uh . . . yes, all right. It can't be any harder on the nerves than what I've just been through.

MISS TATE: We have some roles for the children, too.

KAREN: Could I be an angel?

MISS TATE: Why, I'd be delighted to have you as an angel, Karen. You can be our littlest angel. The girls in the youth group and some of the moms are going to be angels too.

SANDRA: Miss Tate, could I be an angel too, please?

TARA: Oh, come on Sandra, you're not that good an actress.

MRS. GREY *(warning her):* Ta-ra!

MISS TATE: Actually, I was hoping you would be one of the sheep, Sandra. Would that be all right? You get to wear a really cute outfit.

SANDRA: OK. Am I the only sheep?

MISS TATE: No, Kimmie has agreed to be a sheep as well.

BOBBY: Is that all there is in this play, just angels and sheep?

MISS TATE: No, Bobby, we need someone with a good deep voice to be a calf. Do you think you could manage that?

BOBBY: Sure. Mooo . . . Moooooo . . .

MISS TATE *(laughing):* Very good. You're hired!

DUNCAN: What can I be in this play?

PAUL: I think *all* you guys could be little animals—then you wouldn't have to act at all.

MISS TATE: Now, Paul, I think Duncan is a little young to appreciate that kind of humor. Maybe you could be a little donkey, Duncan.

DUNCAN: OK. I'd rather be a little donkey than a big one, anyway. *(Glances at* PAUL. *Some of the young people snicker.)*

MRS. CALDER: All right, you two. That's enough.

MISS TATE: I'll distribute scripts now and we'll have a read-through. Susan, these are for the youth group.

(SUSAN *distributes scripts to the young people and* MISS TATE *distributes scripts to the adults.)*

MISS TATE: Now you'll notice that I've circled a different role on each script. That will indicate the part I would like you to read today.

(The following comments are made as people are receiving their scripts:)

MR. HARPER *(nervously):* My goodness . . . I'm Joseph. I'll never be able to learn all these lines.

JIM *(looking at his own script):* Dad, you only speak four times!

(MR. HARPER *sits shaking his head.)*

ANNE: Oh, good, I get to try the role of the innkeeper's daughter—at least I get to say a few words.

PAUL: Hey, I'm a shepherd. That'll be all right. I was afraid I'd be type-cast as a Wise Man.

IAN: Fat chance, Paul. A wise-guy, maybe.

DUNCAN: Miss Tate, can we wear our costumes?

MISS TATE: No, not today, Duncan.

DUNCAN: But, Miss Tate, I won't feel like a donkey unless I have a costume.

KIMMIE: Could I wear my sheep costume, *please?*

KAREN: I would be a much better angel if I had some wings.

MISS TATE *(hesitating a moment):* All right, we'll compromise. Maybe some simple costuming will make everyone feel more in character. Donkey and sheep, you can wear your ears, and angels you wear your halos and gowns. Shepherds, your robes are in the boxes. They're not labeled yet, so just choose any one today.
(People start to move toward costume boxes.) There are cloaks there for Mary and Joseph as well. Wise Men, you can all wear crowns but there is only one robe there; the others are at the cleaners . . . Anne and Tara, will you help the little ones, please?

(During the costuming, which should be as efficient as possible, smaller children will try out their noises—"moos," "baas," etc. The chairs should be moved back-

stage at this time, too. When TIM *and* DARCY *are dressed—* TIM *will be wearing the only Wise Man's robe—they move to side of stage to watch the first scene. The following conversation should go on while others are still milling about the stage getting ready.)*

TIM *(takes Freddie's box out of his pocket):* OK, Freddie, come on out and watch the play.

DARCY: Aren't you afraid he'll take off?

TIM: No, not with all this commotion. He'll just sit on my sleeve.

DARCY: OK. I can help you keep an eye on him.

MISS TATE *(as the noise dies down):* Everyone set? OK, take your places for the first scene. And, parents, if there are any stage directions you don't understand, just ask one of the youth group members; they've had lots of experience at this. They can interpret for you.

MR. GREY *(looking at the script):* Oh, it can't be that bad.

TRISHA: Miss Tate, are the angels supposed to be on the risers during the entire play?

MISS TATE: Yes, but the lights will be on you only during the shepherds' scene. We need you on stage all the time, as you'll be singing carols in between the scenes.

(MISS TATE *moves down into the audience section to watch the proceedings. In the meantime,* MR. GREY *has seated himself on the floor, downstage left.)*

TARA *(notices where he is):* Dad! What are you doing down *there?*

MR. GREY *(pointing to his script):* Look . . . it says, "Innkeeper sits downstage left."

TARA: Dad, that doesn't mean you sit *down on the stage.* It means . . . no, never mind . . . just come to about here. *(Indicates a place nearby.)*

MISS TATE: All set? Begin Scene One.

CATHY *(Narrator No. 1):* "And it came to pass in those days that there went out a decree from Caesar Augustus, that all the world should be taxed. And all went to be taxed, every one into his own city. And Joseph also went up from Galilee, out of the city of Nazareth into Judea, unto the city of David, which is called Bethlehem."

MR. HARPER *(Joseph):* Ho . . . Ho . . . Ho . . . *(These are said in three different tones as if he is struggling for just the right one. He peers over his glasses at* MISS TATE *after trying each "Ho.")*

MISS TATE: Is there some problem, Mr. Harper?

MR. HARPER: Yes, that word, I'm not sure how you would like me to say it.

26

MISS TATE: Well, it would probably be best if you treated it as a unit with the rest of the sentence—it will make more sense that way. How about saying, "Ho there, innkeeper!"

MR. HARPER: Oh, all right. "Ho there, inkeeper! Before you leave, do you have a room for me and my wife?"

MR. GREY *(innkeeper, he speaks in a monotone):* Eh, what's that you say . . . use this ear.

MISS TATE: A little more expression, Mr. Grey. Mr. Harper, try your line again.

MR. HARPER: "Ho there, innkeeper, before you leave—do you have a room for me and my wife?"

MR. GREY: Eh, what's that you say . . . use this ear.

MR. HARPER: HE YELLS MORE LOUDLY INTO HIS EAR. DO YOU HAVE A ROOM FOR US?

MISS TATE: Oh! Just a second!

MR. HARPER *(hurt):* I thought I used lots of expression, Miss Tate.

MISS TATE: Oh, yes, your expression was wonderful, but you were reading the stage directions. Please don't read the words in brackets.

MR. HARPER: Oh. I see now.

MISS TATE: We'll just carry on from there. First read-throughs are always a little bumpy. Mr. Grey?

MR. GREY *(emphatically):* No, no, no! More rooms. *(Pauses, tries again.)* No. No. No. More rooms? *(Very quickly.)* No no no more rooms! . . . *(Obviously getting exasperated.)* NO, NO! NO MORE ROOMS! *(Suddenly realizes that he has got it right.)* Hey, I think I've got it! I'll just run through that again. No, no . . .

MISS TATE *(quickly):* NO! I mean . . . *(Recovers herself.)* That last one was just about right, Mr. Grey, so I think we'll leave that scene for now and go on to the shepherds' scene. I'd like to be sure everyone gets to try a few lines today. That was a . . . good start, anyway. Thank you. Shepherds, would you like to take your positions?

JAN *(Narrator No. 2):* "And there were, in the same country, shepherds abiding in the field, keeping watch over their flocks by night."

MR. CALDER *(Shepherd No. 1; acting like a nobleman in a Shakespearean play, phony British accent, throwing cloak over his shoulder, etc.):* I say, what a beastly cold night it is! Jolly good thing we brought these extra cloaks, isn't it? *(Looking upward.)* Even the blooming stars seem to be shivering!

(Stunned silence from rest of cast.)

PAUL *(Shepherd No. 4):* Dad! What are you doing?

MR. CALDER: I'm *acting,* what does it look like? I've been dying to try this out for years.

PAUL: But, Dad, this isn't exactly *Hamlet,* you know.

MR. CALDER *(haughtily):* I think we could leave the directing up to the director. What do you think of my interpretation, Miss Tate?

MISS TATE: Well . . . it was certainly dramatic, Mr. Calder. Uh . . . you did add a few words to the script, though. We'll have to look at those extra lines later. For now, I think you could perhaps modify the accent a little . . . the play does take place in the Middle East, you know.

MR. CALDER *(reluctantly):* Well, all right, but it may sound pretty flat without the accent.

MISS TATE: I think we'll chance it. Let's pick up right after Mr. Calder's lines. Shepherd Two . . .

JIM *(Shepherd No. 2):* Shall we gather some wood to make a fire, Father?

MR. CALDER *(Shepherd No. 1):* Yes, go ahead. I think we may need a fire after all.

JIM *(Shepherd No. 2; to Shepherd No. 4):* Come on, Nathan. *(They start to go off, stage left.)*

MR. THOMAS *(Shepherd No. 3):* Those stinkin' sheep are sure restless tonight, aren't they?

MISS TATE *(looking a little panic-stricken):* Excuse me, Mr. Thomas! I don't believe that word was in the script, was it?

MR. THOMAS: "Stinkin'?"

MISS TATE: Yes, that's the one.

MR. THOMAS: Well, I just figure that if Bruce there *(indicating* MR. CALDER) was going to add a couple of words to *his* lines, that I would too. You know, Miss Tate, I've worked as a rancher for 30 years now, and any red-blooded shepherd knows that sheep stink.

MISS TATE *(speaking with some difficulty):* That's a . . . good point, Mr. Thomas, and I do welcome any input that will make the play more realistic. *(Suddenly inspired.)* How about saying "those 'smelly' sheep"? Wouldn't that do?

MR. THOMAS *(reluctantly):* They stink, ma'am. They stink! Do I carry on?

MISS TATE *(a little uncertain):* Uh . . . yes, of course we'll carry on. I think . . . we could let the ladies try a few lines now. Mrs. Walters, if you'll glance ahead a bit, you will see your cue. The Angel Choir will be brightly lit right after Shepherd Three speaks. We'll try it right from Mr. Thomas's line, middle of page 4.

MR. THOMAS: Now . . . where's . . . Oh yeah, here it is . . . Well, let's get the fire started . . . gather 'round so that it's sheltered . . . *(Shepherds begin to do this.)*

MRS. WALTERS *(Head Angel; she says her lines in the tones of a southern evangelical preacher):* Fear not! For behold I bring you good tidings of great joy! Unto you is born this day in the city of David, a Savior which is Christ the Lord! HAL-LE-LU-YAH! *(On this last word, she raises her arms and waves her hands in the air.)*

MISS TATE: Oh, my goodness . . .

MRS. WALTERS *(enthused):* Did you like that, Miss Tate? I got the idea from those TV Crusades.

MISS TATE: That was certainly a . . . unique interpretation, Mrs. Walters. I'm sure you'll . . . get everyone's attention. Now . . . maybe we should move on to that last scene where everyone is involved. This should be the easiest to rehearse as there is no dialogue. Mary, Joseph, and animals, you will be on stage right away and others will enter as indicated. You can check your positions on the diagram. Narrators, I'll just show you where you start . . . *(She goes over to* JAN *and* CATHY *to look at script and others mill around until they are in the correct position. At this point,* DARCY *and* TIM *suddenly realize that Freddie has disappeared. They try to look for him, without attracting the attention of the others.)*

MISS TATE: It looks like everyone's in position. *(She nods in approval as she surveys the group.)* Oh, I think this will be beautiful scene! To set the peaceful mood we're going to have the piano playing softly in the background, while Cathy reads and the animals make their sounds.
(to pianist) _____, are you ready? *(He or she nods.)*

(Music starts, softly at first, but grows louder as the noise level on stage increases.)

CATHY *(Narrator No. 1):* "And the shepherds came with haste and found Mary and Joseph and the Babe . . ."

(During this reading, the animals start to make sounds quietly at first—"moos," "baas," and "hee haws," then they get louder as each wants to be heard above the others. CATHY *tries to read more loudly and ends up shouting and glaring at the little "animals.")*

CATHY *(Narrator No. 1):* "AND ALL THEY THAT HEARD IT WONDERED AT THOSE THINGS WHICH WERE TOLD THEM BY THE SHEP-HERDS . . ."

KIMMIE *(Sheep; yelling loudly):* OUCH! QUIT THAT! *(Begins to hit the donkey who tries to crawl away from the manger. The sheep follows, batting at the donkey all the way.)*

MISS TATE: What is going on there?

BOBBY *(calf):* The donkey was biting the sheep!

MRS. WALTERS *(Head Angel; as she rushes down from the risers):* Kimmie, darling! Are you all right?

(KIMMIE *wails loudly, but keeps batting at the donkey.)*

MRS. WALTERS: You bad boy, biting little girls like that.

MR. CALDER *(Shepherd No. 1):* I don't think he would have bit her if she hadn't been making faces at him.

KIMMIE: I was just trying to look like a sheep.

DUNCAN *(Donkey):* Well, I was just trying to bite like a donkey.

MRS. WALTERS: Imagine a parent defending behavior like that! The child deserves to be spanked.

MR. CALDER: I think I can discipline my son without asking for advice.

MR. THOMAS *(Shepherd No. 3):* OUCH! What was that? *(Puts hands over a spot on his arm and rubs it.)*

MR. CALDER *(Shepherd No. 1):* OW! Something just bit me! *(Slaps his leg.)*

MRS. BAXTER *(Mary):* Ohhhhh! *(Jumps up indignantly, hand on her hip.)* Jonathan Harper! I'm shocked!

MR. HARPER *(Joseph; looking around, bewildered):* What did I do?

TIM *(rushing onstage in his Wise Man's crown and robe):* Wait! Quit swatting, everybody! It's just Freddie!

MR. THOMAS *(Shepherd No. 3; looking at his script, puzzled):* I didn't know there was a Freddie in this play.

MISS TATE *(suddenly understanding; she is almost totally exasperated now):* Oh, it's that flea!

MRS. WALTERS *(shocked):* The boy has *fleas?*

MISS TATE: No, not *fleas.* Just *one* flea.

MRS. WALTERS: Well, where is it? *(Looks around nervously.)*

MISS TATE: I don't know. Tim? (TIM *is busy examining the bottom of* MR. CALDER*'s trousers.)*

TIM: I'm looking, Miss Tate. I don't want him to get squashed. Oh, there he goes! Stand still, Mrs. Walters.

(TIM *quickly puts butterfly net over her glasses. She screams.)*

TIM: Ha. Got him. That was close. *(Reproachfully to* MRS. WALTERS.) You almost scared him away.

MRS. WALTERS *(weakly):* I need a chair.

(MR. HARPER *gets one for her.*)

MISS TATE *(trying to be patient):* Tim, did you release that flea on purpose?

TIM: Well, not exactly. I just thought Freddie would enjoy watching some of the action.

MISS TATE: Well, he can *watch* the action, but I don't really want him to be *part* of it. I'm afraid Freddie has got to go. He's far too disruptive.

TIM: I guess you're right. I'll leave him at home from now on.

MISS TATE *(with relief):* Good. *(To the others)* Well, I think we've all had quite enough for one practice. Maybe we'll stop here and get a fresh start at the next rehearsal. How does that sound?

(VARIOUS PEOPLE: Sure. OK. We'll be here. Etc.)

MISS TATE: Will the Youth Group stay behind a few minutes to clean up?

MRS. CALDER *(as people go offstage):* I enjoyed that more than I ever would have guessed, Miss Tate. Do you think all the rehearsals will be as exciting as this one?

MISS TATE: Quite frankly, Mrs. Calder, I sort of hope they're not.

MR. THOMAS: It's gonna be a great play, Miss Tate. I'll tell all my friends. This is one funny Nativity Pageant. They're usually so serious.

MISS TATE: Well, we really weren't trying for humor, Mr. Thomas.

MR. THOMAS *(pleasantly surprised):* You don't say? Imagine us bein' that funny with just one rehearsal.

MISS TATE *(with a weak laugh):* Yes, imagine.

(Everyone exits down through audience. They could adlib lines to one another as they go out. Several of the young people crowd around Miss Tate, while others stack chairs, pack costumes, etc.)

MARJ: Miss Tate, what are we going to *do?*

MISS TATE: Do?

MARJ: About the parents! They're going to *ruin* our play!

TIM: The audience is gonna crack right up when they hear those wild accents.

JAN: And don't forget the little animals. There's going to be pinching and fighting during the Manger Scene when everything's supposed to be peaceful.

MISS TATE: Whoa, now, just a minute. Let's not get carried away here. This was just the first rehearsal, remember, and you're assuming on the basis of one practice that the cast can't handle their roles! If I had done that a couple of years ago, this youth group would never have produced a single play. You people used to be terrible on your first read-throughs.

31

TIM: Us?

PAUL *(in disbelief):* Not me, Miss Tate!

MISS TATE: Especially you!

IAN: I guess she fixed your little red wagon, Paul.

MISS TATE: *Everybody* was in the same "little red wagon," Ian. All of you had to work hard to improve your acting technique, and it's paying off. We've put on some good plays, haven't we?

(There is a brief silence as kids glance at one another.)

CINDY: Yes, we have, Miss Tate. And look, you guys, maybe it's time we did some backup work and let somebody else be the stars for a change.

MARJ: Oh, Cindy, quit being so noble!

(General laughter from the others.)

MISS TATE: Cindy does have a point. And if your parents see you tackling your *minor* roles with lots of enthusiasm, I'm sure they'll work harder than ever to do a good job on their roles.

JIM: I suppose we could help them at home with lines, rather than just complaining about how they say them.

MISS TATE: Right! That would be a help to me, too.

DARCY: But what about the little twerps? How are we going to get *them* to take their scene seriously? They seem to think the stage is some kind of jungle gym.

MISS TATE: Well, maybe it's our interpretation of the manger scene that's wrong.

CINDY: What do you mean?

MISS TATE: Maybe we're expecting the manger scene to be too perfect. I have to admit when we started that scene today, I wanted the calf to "moo" just the right way, not too loud, not too soft. And I assumed that the sheep would wait until the cow finished before they started to "baa." And that's silly when you really stop to think about it. It just wouldn't have happened that way.

CINDY: Hey, that's right! There's always lots of noises and shuffling going on in our stables.

MISS TATE: So you see what I'm getting at then? God purposely chose a less than ideal setting for the birth of His Son, and here we are, trying to transform it into the Stable Hilton, complete with soft music and perfectly behaved little animals.

TARA: So don't worry about it if the kids start to attack one another?

MISS TATE: Hopefully it won't get that bad.

PAUL: Maybe we could tie them to the manger!

MISS TATE: I hope you're not serious.

PAUL: Well . . . no, I guess not.

MISS TATE *(very earnestly):* I guess what I'm really asking you all to believe is that participation is more important than perfection. I know we could have a nearly perfect play by doing it ourselves, but by including the parents and little kids, we're not only sharing the spotlight, but we're giving them a wonderful chance to experience the Christmas story first-hand.

PAUL: I've got a great idea, Miss Tate! Let's rename our play so that no one is misled! We could call it, "The Not Too Perfect Nativity Play"!

MISS TATE *(laughing):* We'll see about that. Are you all game to give this your best effort even if the end result isn't perfect?

(VARIOUS ANSWERS: Sure. OK. It'll be fun. Etc.)

TIM: Miss Tate, if we're not trying for perfection, does that mean Freddie can be in the play after all? *(Sees look on* MISS TATE*'s face.)* Just kidding.

MARJ: Look, Tim, a mediocre play, I can grow to accept, but I don't intend to be part of a fiasco!

TIM: All right, all right. I'll keep him at home.

MISS TATE: Good. And don't worry, Marj. The parents and kids will do a fine job.

MARJ: I hope you're right.

MISS TATE: Will you turn out the lights as you leave, Paul. I'll get the backstage ones.

PAUL: Sure thing. Let's kill the lights you guys! Ahhhhhhh . . . eeee . . . ahhh!

(He does karate chops and leaps along the aisle as he goes out.)

(The others follow him, laughing. MISS TATE *remains on stage alone for a few seconds. She looks upward for her last line.)*

MISS TATE: And now, dear Lord, please let me be right!

Act II

(There is lots of activity on stage: sets and props are being arranged, a couple of the "animals" are on the risers, MR. GREY *is practicing "walking" with his cane. He acts and speaks like an old man for the duration of the play, and is obviously very much "into" his role.* MR. HARPER, *too, is pacing the stage but in a nervous,*

33

erratic manner. He is studying his script, looking up occasionally to mutter lines. TARA *appears from backstage.)*

TARA: Dad, you're wanted back in the makeup room for a few minutes. The girls would like to put some more powder in your hair.

MR. GREY: Eh? What's that you say?

TARA: Dad, will you cut that out! You heard exactly what I said.

MR. GREY: Kids nowadays! No respect for their elders. Next thing you know they'll be trying to tell the preists how to run the Temple.

MISS TATE *(coming onstage):* Hello, Mr. Grey. How are you tonight?

MR. GREY: Eh? Speak up young lady!

MISS TATE: HOW ARE YOU FEELING TONIGHT?

MR. GREY: Oh, fair, just fair. Old age, you know . . . it's a killer.

MISS TATE: You have really perfected that walk now.

MR. GREY: Eh?

MISS TATE: NEVER MIND. JUST CARRY ON.

TARA *(as* MR. GREY *hobbles off towards the makeup room):* Miss Tate! He's driving our whole family crazy. We're beginning to wonder if he will ever come back to the 20th century.

MISS TATE: Well, hopefully he'll be back after tonight's performance. He is doing a wonderful job of his role, you know.

TARA: Well, he *should* be good at it. He acts deaf for 24 hours a day and now everyone in the house is shouting at one another. It's awful.

(MR. THOMAS *has come onstage from the makeup room and looks rather glum.)*

MR. THOMAS: Miss Tate, I don't know if I'm ever going to live this down.

MISS TATE: What's the problem, Mr. Thomas?

MR. THOMAS: All my friends seein' me in this *makeup.* I'm probably the first rancher in my district to wear lipstick.

MISS TATE: Don't worry too much about it. Even John Wayne had to wear makeup when he acted.

MR. THOMAS: You don't say! OK! I guess if it was good enough for the Duke, it's good enough for me.

(MRS. WALTERS *enters from back of auditorium. She is singing "Joy to the World" with great gusto.)*

MR. THOMAS *(calls out when she stops at the end of a line for breath):* You're late, Beatrice.

MRS. WALTERS: Oh no I'm not. Besides, I've already done my own makeup at home. Can't you see my *Mary Kay* glow?

MR. THOMAS: It's not good enough, you know. Miss Tate here was sayin' last night when she saw you under the lights that you looked all washed up.

MRS. WALTERS *(stops in her tracks):* Washed UP!

MISS TATE: Oh, Mr. Thomas! The expression I used was washed OUT, not up!

MR. THOMAS: Oh well, excuse me.

MISS TATE *(to* MRS. WALTERS*):* But you do need some stage makeup, though. The lights are very bright. Just go on into the back. The girls are expecting you.

(MRS. WALTERS, *in a bit of a huff, goes backstage.* MR. HARPER*'s muttering gets louder as she exits.)*

MR. THOMAS: Now there's a sad case.

(They both look over at MR. HARPER *who has put down his script and now appears to be reading something on the inside of his arm.)*

MISS TATE: What on earth is he doing?

MR. THOMAS: He's cheatin', that's what. He's got all his lines written on the inside of his arm. I saw 'em in the makeup room.

MISS TATE: Oh dear. And he doesn't even need them. He *knows* his lines. I'd better go over and give him a big of encouragement. Mr. Harper . . .

MR. HARPER *(jumping nervously):* What! Are we starting already?

MISS TATE: No, no. Not yet. Just come backstage with me for a second. I'd like to talk to you.

(They go off to side of stage. MRS. BAXTER *and* MRS. CALDER *enter from backstage.)*

MRS. BAXTER: Well, I don't care what you see in all the pictures, Doreen, I don't believe Mary rode a donkey anywhere. No pregnant woman in her right mind would even dream of getting up on a donkey. I have enough trouble getting in and out of the car.

MRS. CALDER: Well, it was a good idea . . . if we had just been able to locate a donkey. Just think how realistic it would have looked.

MRS. BAXTER: Humph. Well, walking is realistic, too, and a whole lot more comfortable. Let's sit down for a minute.

(As MRS. BAXTER *is awkwardly getting a chair,* MISS TATE *enters and spies her white nursing-style shoes.)*

35

MISS TATE: Oh, Mrs. Baxter, I forgot to tell you yesterday, those shoes are much too modern. I brought a pair of sandals for you. They're in the dressing room.

MRS. BAXTER: You've got to be kidding. Not those lace-up things! (MISS TATE *nods.*) Oh well . . . *(Sighing.)* If someone will just tell me where my feet are, I'll see what I can do.

MRS. CALDER: Come on, Betty, I'll do it for you. *(They exit backstage.)*

(MRS. GREY *enters from backstage and seems to be in a kind of daze.)*

MISS TATE: Hi, Mrs. Grey. Are you feeling better now?

MRS. GREY *(stares straight ahead):* Right now, I don't feel anything, fortunately. I am completely numb. If someone will just point me in the direction of the risers?

MISS TATE: We have about 15 minutes left before we start, you know.

MRS. GREY *(should be said slowly and evenly, with a trancelike quality):* Fine, fine. I'm going to go to the risers, and I'm going to stay there from now until the end of the play, and then I am going to come down off the risers, and then I am never, *ever* going to go on stage again.

MISS TATE: Oh, you're going to do just fine. Don't worry!

MRS. GREY: The risers?

MISS TATE: Over this way . . . *(Turns her around and steers her over to the risers.)* And Jan, I think we should close the curtains now. There are already a lot of people waiting out in the hall.

(Curtain closes. Podium is moved outside the curtain, stage right. CATHY *and* JAN *may test the mike, organize their papers, etc. After they go back behind the curtain,* MR. THOMAS's *head appears at center crack of curtain.)*

MR. THOMAS *(whistles):* Will you look at all those people!

CINDY *(from behind curtain):* Dad! What are you doing? Come back behind the curtain!

MR. THOMAS: Oh, it's OK. It's pretty dark out there.

CINDY: Well, the *audience* may be in the dark, but *you're* not. Come on! *(Head disappears.)*

(Pianist enters and plays carols for two or three minutes.)

(Spotlight on MISS TATE *as she enters and stands behind podium. She speaks to the audience.)*

MISS TATE: Good evening, everyone, and welcome to the youth group's presentation of the Nativity Play. This year, we invited entire families to participate in the production of our play, so you will be seeing a combined cast of parents, teens, and children. We are all hoping that our presentation will be enjoyable and meaningful for each one of you. Thank you.

(She goes behind curtain and the "Nativity Play" begins.)

The Nativity Play

(ANGEL CHORUS *on risers at back of stage and remains there throughout the Nativity Play. They sing carols in between scenes and may be dimly lit for this. At all other times—except during the "appearance" to the shepherds—they should be "invisible." This could be done either by having them situated behind a scrim, or by using spotlights and keeping action in the scenes to the front of the stage, so that the upstage area can be dark. Chorus will sing first two verses of each carol unless otherwise indicated.)*

CHOIR: "O Little Town of Bethlehem" (or similar)

NARRATOR No. 1: "And it came to pass in those days, that there went out a decree from Caesar Augustus that all the world should be taxed, every one into his own city. And Joseph also went up from Galilee, out of the city of Nazareth, into Judea, unto the city of David, which is called Bethlehem, to be taxed with Mary, his espoused wife, being great with child."

(Spotlight on INNKEEPER, *who is seated at a small rough table, downstage left. He is just getting up to leave and picks up his cane and a purse of money.* MARY *and* JOSEPH *enter from stage right.* JOSEPH *calls to him.)*

JOSEPH: Ho there, inkeeper! Before you go in, do you have a room for me and my wife?

INNKEEPER *(very hard of hearing):* Eh? What's that you say? Speak up! *(Tilts head toward* JOSEPH *to give him his good ear.)*

JOSEPH *(yelling more loudly into his ear):* DO YOU HAVE A ROOM FOR US?

INNKEEPER: No, No. No more rooms. I have just rented the last one. *(Jingles his purse of coins.)*

JOSEPH: But we're desperate—we've been traveling for days. Surely you have some place . . .

INNKEEPER *(tilting head again):* What's that you say? Speak up!

GRANDDAUGHTER *(entering from stage left):* What's going on, Grandpa? *(Sees* MARY *and* JOSEPH.) Oh, not more travelers! *(Regretfully.)* And we have no place for them!

JOSEPH: Good child, is there not some place—a backroom, some sort of shelter? My wife is expecting a baby and has not had a decent rest for days!

GRANDDAUGHTER *(to* MARY): Oh, you poor woman. *(Suddenly alarmed.)* Is the baby to arrive soon?

37

MARY: I'm sure it could be any day now.

GRANDDAUGHTER *(thoughtfully):* And the traveling may speed things up . . . we must do something . . . *(Excited.)* Wait! I have an idea! What about the stable? It's at least warm and dry. What do you think, Grandpa? *(Looks at him but he obviously has not heard.)* WHAT ABOUT THE STABLE?

INNKEEPER: Well, if they are satisfied . . .

MARY: Oh yes. I'll be grateful for any place as long as I can rest.

GRANDDAUGHTER: All right, that's settled then. I'll get my brother to take out some fresh straw and some blankets. Come with me first, though, and have something to eat.

(Blackout as they go offstage left.)

NARRATOR NO. 2: "And so it was, that, while they were there, the days were accomplished that she should be delivered. And she brought forth her first-born son, and wrapped him in swaddling clothes and laid him in a manger; because there was no room for them in the inn."

CHOIR: "Once in Royal David's City" (or similar)

NARRATOR NO. 2: "And there were in the same country, shepherds abiding in the field, keeping watch over their flocks by night . . ."

CHOIR: "The First Noel"

(Lights up on SHEPHERDS, *stage right.* SHEPHERDS NO. 2 *and* NO. 4 *are seated. Beside them are a couple of bundles of wood.* SHEPHERDS NO. 1 *and* NO. 3 *are slowly packing, holding their cloaks close.)*

SHEPHERD NO. 1: What a beastly cold night it is! It's a good thing we brought these extra cloaks. *(Looks up.)* Even the stars seem to be shivering . . .

SHEPHERD NO. 2 *(jumping up):* Shall we gather some kindling to make a fire, Father?

SHEPHERD NO. 1: Yes, go ahead. I think we may need one after all.

SHEPHERD NO. 2 *(to the other boy):* Come on, Nathan! *(They go offstage.)*

SHEPHERD NO. 3 *(as he and* SHEPHERD NO. 1 *begin to arrange the wood for the fire):* Those stinkin' sheep are sure restless tonight. It makes me nervous, even though we've seen no sign of wolves around here.

SHEPHERD NO. 1: Maybe they can sense the mood of all those travelers in Bethlehem. Everyone's nerves are really on edge these past few days. I don't think even the Roman authorities had any idea how many people were going to crowd into little Bethlehem. The inns are full, every home is packed with relatives . . . and apparently there are still more to come. And somehow . . . everyone is supposed to be housed and fed. *(Shakes his head.)*

SHEPHERD NO. 3: Well, I'll be glad when all the noise and activity settles down. if I wanted all this madness, I'd be living in Jerusalem.

(Boys reappear, carrying sticks, dried grasses, etc.)

SHEPHERD NO. 1: Looks like you were successful. These should be just enough to get a blaze started.

SHEPHERD NO. 3: Do you feel that breeze? Odd time of night for a wind to come up. It's been so peaceful . . . *(All* SHEPHERDS *look around a bit, and up at the sky)* . . . well, let's get this fire started. *(Kneels down to arrange kindling.)* Gather 'round so it's sheltered . . .

(Suddenly ANGEL CHORUS *is illuminated.* SHEPHERDS *fall to the ground and shield their eyes.)*

HEAD ANGEL: "Fear not, for behold I bring you good tidings of great joy which shall be to all people. Unto you is born this day in the City of David, a Savior, which is Christ the Lord. Hallelujah! And this shall be a sign unto you: you shall find the babe wrapped in swaddling clothes, lying in a manger."

ENTIRE ANGEL CHORUS *(spoken triumphantly):* "Glory to God in the highest, and on earth peace, good will toward men!" (CHORUS *sings "Angels We Have Heard on High" [or similar] and lights fade.* SHEPHERDS *slowly rise.)*

SHEPHERD NO. 4 *(in awe):* Father, I can hardly believe what we have just seen!

SHEPHERD NO. 3 *(slowly):* All these years, our priests and leaders have waited for some sign from God—some direct word from Him—and it comes to *us,* simple shepherds?

SHEPHERD NO. 1: Surely God does work in mysterious ways. This must be the arrival of the Savior that Isaiah wrote about.

SHEPHERD NO. 3 *(incredulously):* But in a manger? What kind of a ruler would be born in a manger?

SHEPHERD NO. 1: Who are *we* to question God's decisions? *(Urgently.)* Come on, let us hurry to do what the angel commanded.

SHEPHERD NO. 2: But Father, the sheep . . .

SHEPHERD NO. 1: They'll be fine. Let's go, quickly!

(All exit, stage left. Blackout.)

*(Piano music or soloist: one verse of "O Holy Night," lights up on the manger scene [*MARY, JOSEPH, *and the* BABE], *at conclusion of song.)*

*(*CHOIR *sings "Away in a Manger," two verses, then the pianist will play one extra verse while the* CHOIR *hums softly and animals make their sounds.* NARRATOR NO. 1 *begins reading when music and sounds stop.)*

39

NARRATOR NO. 1: "And the shepherds came with haste and found Mary and Joseph and the Babe lying in a manger." (SHEPHERDS *enter, stage left, and kneel by the manger.*) "And when the shepherds saw Him they made known the saying which was told them concerning this child. And all they that heard it wondered at those things which were told them by the shepherds. But Mary kept all these things and pondered them in her heart."

(CHOIR *sings "Silent Night," 3 verses.*)

NARRATOR NO. 2: "Now when Jesus was born in Bethlehem of Judea in the days of Herod the King, behold there came wise men from the East, following a star." *(Instrumental music: "We Three Kings")* "And lo, the star went before them till it came and stood over where the young child was. And when they were come into the place, they saw the child with Mary, his mother, and fell and worshiped him. And when they had opened their treasures, they presented unto him gifts—gold, and frankincense and myrrh." (WISE MEN *have entered and presented their gifts.*)

(CHOIR *sings last verse of "We Three Kings"—"Glorious now . . ."*)

NARRATOR NO. 1 *(these next lines to be read triumphantly):* "And in this way the prophecy of Isaiah came to be fulfilled: For unto us a child is born, unto us a son is given, and the government shall be upon his shoulder and his name shall be called Wonderful Counselor, the Almighty God, the Everlasting Father, the Prince of Peace!"

(CHOIR *sings "Joy to the World." Curtain closes after this song.*)

(MISS TATE *comes out and stands between the two* NARRATORS.)

MISS TATE: I'd like to thank all of you for coming out tonight to join in our celebration of the anniversary of Christ's birth. On behalf of the young people and their families, I wish you a peaceful and happy Christmas. Thank you.

(MISS TATE *and girls exit. Pianist plays one verse of "O Come All Ye Faithful" and then goes backstage as well.*)

(*The curtain opens after a few seconds. Some kids are congratulating parents, some are removing sets and props, others go to dressing rooms.*)

CINDY *(to her father):* That was really good, Dad. I was proud of you.

MR. THOMAS: Well, it sure wasn't perfect, but I guess it was OK.

MARJ: It was better than OK, Mr. Thomas! And, besides, nobody was expecting it to be perfect!

CINDY: *Nobody?*

MARJ: Well . . . almost nobody. You did a very good job of your role, anyway.

MR. THOMAS: I enjoyed the whole thing except for this makeup business. Where do I get this stuff off—same room as before? *(Starts backstage.)*

CINDY: That's right, Dad. See you later.

(JAN comes quickly on stage, enters through audience as if she has just come from the foyer. She appears to be quite excited.)

JAN: You guys should hear all the comments out in the hall! The audience *loved* the play!

CINDY: You sound surprised.

JAN: Well, aren't you? I had no idea it would turn out so well.

MARJ: Neither did I. When I think of some of those rehearsals . . .

(MISS TATE enters stage left.)

MISS TATE: You girls had better hurry up and get changed. I ordered the pizza and it will be in the lounge in 15 minutes.

MARJ: I don't think we'll need any, Miss Tate. We've eaten already.

MISS TATE: You have?

MARJ: Yeah, we've been eating our words.

MISS TATE: Oh . . . I see. No bitter taste, I hope.

JAN: Not at all. We've actually had a good time, eh, Marj?

MARJ: Yeah, that's right.

MISS TATE: Thank you for all your hard work.

MARJ: It was worth it. See you in the lounge!

(Girls exit backstage. MISS TATE is left standing alone on stage. She looks upward once more.)

MISS TATE: And thank YOU, too!

Star Track

"Just Another Child"

by Lori Taylor and David Carter

Dedication
For SONLIGHT
Trinity United Methodist Church
Gainesville, Fla.

Cast of Characters:

SAM GOLDSTEIN: *an ambitious, investigative newspaper reporter*
RHONDA WUNDERBURGHER: *a brassy, young newspaper photographer*
BALTHAZAR: *the gracious leader of the three kings*
GASPAR: *a distinguished but rather impatient king*
MELCHIOR: *a travel-weary old king, full of aches and pains*
SALOME: *the glamorous, diabolical sister of Herod*
HIGH PRIEST: *ignorant and totally corrupt*
JOSHUA: *an arrogant priest and teacher with little knowledge*
JACOB: *a stammering student priest*
ETHEL, SYLVIA, BLANCHE: *shepherdesses who are anxious to relate their stories*
STAN: *a village shepherd*
(EXTRAS: *an assortment of peasants, Pharisees, merchants, villagers, etc.*)

Scenes:

Scene 1: A Jerusalem marketplace
Scene 2: Herod's palace
Scene 3A: Temple courtyard
Scene 3B: A room in the temple
Scene 4: Shepherds' village
Scene 5: Outside the Bethlehem stable

Production Note:

The scenes above may be set very impressionistically. A prop or two indicating a location are all that is needed.

Music Suggestions:

Throughout this script there are places where suggested music may be inserted.

Scene 1: A Marketplace in Jerusalem

(As the scene opens, there are street people standing around as a crowd; a leper shouts "unclean"; merchants sell wares; Pharisees pose piously; etc. RHONDA *enters, taking pictures of the crowds.)*

SAM: Hey, Rhonda, over here! Get a good shot of this guy begging.

RHONDA: I got one already. We've got enough of the marketplace, Sam. All we need is one good interview, and we've got it made.

SAM: Right. Let's find a wealthy family and play up their contrast to this miserable bunch of "low-lifes." You know what I mean . . . Headline: "Caesar Augustus Decrees a Census!" "Census Brings Rich to Their Senses!" or "Filth and Poverty Clash with Cash!"

RHONDA: Yeah! Maybe if we're lucky, we can cash in on some of that cash ourselves! Sounds great, Sam. I like that angle. Now if we could just find someone who fits that description.

SAM: Look for someone with lots of jewelry . . . *(Looks around.)* Ahhh, wait a minute. I think I see exactly what we need. Whoa . . . would ya' look at those three dudes coming up the road? I think we've got more than we bargained for here. They've got wealth coming out of their ears!

RHONDA: Those are crowns on their heads! Sam . . . they're kings! And they look foreign. They sure don't look like they were born here in Jerusalem. I wonder why they came here during the census?

SAM: I don't know, but I'm gonna find out. I've got a hunch this may be the scoop we've been looking for! Follow me, and just go along with everything I say. *(Walks toward* KINGS *and bows elaborately.)* Good afternoon, Your Kingships. Welcome to our fair city. I am Sam Goldstein, and this is Rhonda Wunderburgher. We're doing a series of articles about the census. We represent the *Jerusalem Post.* Have you by any chance been following it?

BALTHAZAR: Why no. We've been following the *Star.*

SAM: Hmmmm . . . the "Star"? *(To* RHONDA*)* I didn't know *that* paper was also taking an in-depth look at the situation. *(To* KINGS*)* I'll have to take a look at a copy of it.

MELCHIOR: But there *is* no copy of it.

SAM: Why not?

GASPAR: It's unlike anything we've ever seen before.

SAM: But you haven't read *my* . . .

BALTHAZAR: It'll be the biggest story to hit the face of the earth!

SAM: Well, of course, I modestly feel that *my* story would outshine anything . . .

GASPAR: Nothing outshines this!

SAM *(growing very impatient, to* RHONDA): What is he? Some kind of *wise guy?*

RHONDA: Uh . . . what my partner is trying to say is that we are striving for excellence in our own reporting, and would very much like to interview Your Highnesses. We feel it would add a new *richness (Nudged by* SAM.) . . . er . . . a quality to our writing.

SAM: Sir, if you would just consider letting us draw you away from the "Star," we would like to have the exclusive story of . . . *(Elaborate gesture)* Your Worships.

BALTHAZAR *(confused):* But . . . our *worship* is directly *related* to the Star.

SAM: Why? Are you uncles of the editor, or something?

GASPAR *(to* MELCHIOR): What *is* he talking about? Do you think *all* the citizens of Jerusalem make so little sense? *(To* BALTHAZAR) Let's move on, Balthazar. We must reach Herod's palace by nightfall. We'd better hurry.

SAM: Herod? You're on your way to visit King Herod? *(Looks excitedly at* RHONDA.)

MELCHIOR: Why, yes. Do you know him?

SAM: Know him? *Know him? (Laughs evasively.)* Why, we'd be glad to escort you to the palace. *(Exchanges glances with* RHONDA.)

RHONDA: Providing, of course, that you'll reconsider telling *us* the exciting details of your travel.

BALTHAZAR: We would be most happy to recount the story. In fact, we plan to tell it to the whole world.

SAM: Well, then the *Jerusalem Post* is the newspaper to do it.

BALTHAZAR: A *newspaper?* Ah, yes, now I understand. Fine. Fine. Now lead the way to the palace. You may take notes while we speak to Herod of this matter.

(Blackout.)

Scene 2: Herod's Palace

(There is a dinner party in progress.)

*(*SERVANT *enters and whispers in* HEROD's *ear.)*

HEROD *(claps hands):* All right everyone! Knock it off! I've just been informed that we have some rather impressive company. Apparently, three kings have traveled quite a long way to talk to me. No doubt they've heard about my extensive building program.

MAN *(secretly from the crowd):* Or maybe they came to discuss your human disposal plan!

HEROD: Who said that? Who said that? I'll have you know I take great pride in all my "disposals." And if you're not careful, there may be a few more!

SALOME: Now, Harry, don't start getting paranoid again. I'm sure he didn't mean anything by that remark.

HEROD: Oh, all right. Let's see what our visitors want. Send them in.

(Trumpet fanfare, followed by a grand procession up to HEROD's *throne.)*

SAM: Your Herodness, Goldstein and Wunderburgher here. *Jerusalem Post. (Elaborate bow.)* We would like to present three illustrious colleagues of yours: King Balthazar, King Melchior, and King Gaspar. *(To the* KINGS*)* This is Herod the Great and his sister, Salome. *(To* HEROD.*)* Your Majesty, they have a most unusual story to tell you.

RHONDA: They have agreed to let the *Post* cover it exclusively. With your permission, I'd like to get a few pictures of you standing next to them.

HEROD: By all means. Stand over here, though. This is my better side.

BALTHAZAR: Sir, thank you for seeing us on such short notice. We do indeed have a most incredible story to tell.

MELCHIOR: Please sit down again and make yourself comfortable. We've been riding camels for the past several weeks, and we'd just as soon stand for a while.

SALOME: Tell us, my good man, what brings you three to Jerusalem during this chaotic time? Surely not the census!

GASPAR: No, we're here because we're following a very special star.

HEROD: Oh, yes. Well, now that you've found me, how can I be of help to you wise gentlemen? Would you like my autograph?

BALTHAZAR: No, you have unfortunately misunderstood. We are not looking for *you;* we are looking for a king.

SALOME: But my brother *is* a *king.* What do you mean by this insult?

GASPAR: We are following a star that is leading us to the long-awaited Messiah. The King of Kings.

HEROD: But *I* am the King of Kings? Isn't that right, everybody?

CROWD: Yes! Right! Absolutely! *(etc.)*

HEROD: You see? They love me. *(To* SALOME*)* . . . if they know what's good for 'em!

BALTHAZAR: But sir, with all due respect, we are not looking for *you*. We are looking for a tiny baby that has just been born. He is somewhere in this region, and we have come to worship Him.

SALOME: A baby? A baby? You've come all this way to find a baby?

HEROD: Hey, it sounds like just another kid to me. What's the big deal?

GASPAR: Oh, I assure you, He's not just another *(Distastefully)* "kid." As we've been trying to explain, we believe this child is the Messiah. The One the world has been waiting for for centuries. Surely you've heard of "Emmanuel."

HEROD: Ah, yes, of course. *(With a puzzled look at* SALOME.*)* Well, it appears as though you've captured the interest of my people. Perhaps you won't mind answering a few of their questions, while I confer with my sister for a few moments.

(KINGS *nod consent, while the "party" closes in on them,* SAM *and* RHONDA *overhear the following conversation.)*

HEROD *(to* SALOME): But he's no son of *mine*, so how could he possibly be a king?

SALOME: I don't like this, Harry. This could threaten your whole line of descendants. We must look into this matter thoroughly *(Menacingly.)* . . . if you know what I mean.

HEROD: Yes, I think I catch your drift. Sounds like an excellent opportunity for a little more population control. I'll send those reporters to find out if this kid really exists. If so, then I'll just order a clean sweep, so to speak, of all boys in that general area under two years of age. *(Crosses to* KINGS.*)* Yes, this story is most exciting, and I too feel the need to bow down to this extraordinary babe. Might I suggest that you freshen up after your long journey.

SALOME: Our servants will take care of your every need.

HEROD: Yes, and while you're resting, I'll send our two reporter friends to investigate the situation for us. I believe they should begin their search in the reference room at the Great Temple. We have many learned scholars there. Perhaps the Scriptures can tell them where to find this child.

MELCHIOR: An excellent idea, my friend!

HEROD: Naturally. I will let you know as soon as they bring back some news of the child's whereabouts.

KINGS *(ad lib):* Fine. Good. etc.

(KINGS *exit with a few servants.* SAM *and* RHONDA *follow close behind, but are recalled by* HEROD.*)*

HEROD: Oh . . . you there! Reporters! Come here!

SAM *(frightened):* Y-y-y-you wish to speak to us, O Mighty One?

RHONDA: We just thought we should go with them to . . . uh . . . freshen up.

HEROD: No, that won't be necessary. I have a little proposition for you two.

RHONDA: Proposition?

HEROD: There's a great deal of money involved, if you play your cards right. I want you to do some research for me about this . . . this . . . "king."

RHONDA: Uh . . . I'm not sure our chief would let us take any time off right now. He expects several more color features about the Census.

SALOME: I assure you, there'll be lots of *color* in *this* story.

HEROD *(laughing):* Yeah, *red!* Uh, yes . . . *"read"* by thousands of my people. I will speak to your editor about this assignment. And I will pay you handsomely for reporting everything to me first, before you print it. *(Tosses* SAM *a purse of coins.)* Here, this will get you started. Agreed?

SAM: Agreed. We will be most honored to serve you.

RHONDA: But Sam . . .

SAM *(aside):* What harm can it do?

RHONDA: I don't want to be a part of this baby killing!

SAM: Look, Herod's plan will go through whether we work with him or not. *You* were the one who wanted to get rich quick, remember? Well, now's our chance.

RHONDA: I guess you're right. But I still don't like it one bit.

SAM: Sire, we're at your disposal. *(Bows.)*

MAN: Don't ever say that to Herod the Great! He'll take you up on it!

HEROD: Who said that? Who said that?

(Blackout.)

Scene 3A:
Pharisees and Jews in Outer Courtyard of the Temple

(CROWD *ad-libs courtyard "hubbub."* SAM *and* RHONDA *enter.* RHONDA *starts to follow* SAM *into the Temple.)*

GUARD: Excuse me, miss, but you can't go in there. Only men are permitted.

RHONDA: Huh? Oh, yeah, I almost forgot. Sam, I'll wait out here.

SAM: Right. I'll take care of this as quickly as possible.

(Blackout.)

Scene 3B: Reference Room in the Temple

JOSHUA: Jacob, you're a mess. Your shoes are scruffy; your robe's dirty. And when did you last get your hair cut?

JACOB: I've just come from the sanctuary. It was *my* turn on the night shift!

HIGH PRIEST: And your hair grew *that* long during one night, I suppose?

JACOB: Well, no, I . . .

(A bell is heard at the door.)

HIGH PRIEST: Oh, never mind. Jacob, go and see who's at the door.

(JACOB *exits.)*

HIGH PRIEST: Will that boy ever make a priest?

JOSHUA: I must admit, my lord, he's an excellent student. He remembers every word of my lectures.

HIGH PRIEST: Maybe, but I think . . .

(JACOB *returns with* SAM.)

SAM: Your High Priestus . . . please forgive this intrusion upon your studies. I have been sent by Herod. Do I have your permission to speak?

HIGH PRIEST: By Herod, you say? But of course . . . *(Sticks out his hand for an expected bribe.)* I'm all *ears.*

(Sam *begrudgingly dips into the purse once, and then again until the* HIGH PRIEST *is satisfied. He mumbles to* JACOB.)

SAM: Looks like all *hands,* to me. They don't make high priests like they used to.

JACOB: That's for sure!

HIGH PRIEST *(finishing the transaction):* Well, now that you have my full attention, what can we do for you?

SAM: Three kings from the East have come to the palace asking all sorts of questions about some baby. Herod thinks you can help.

HIGH PRIEST *(confused):* Yes, of course, but, how?

SAM: They have traveled for many weeks, looking for a child whose birth has been marked by the appearance of a new star. They have tracked the star here, and are asking where the baby may have been born.

JOSHUA: Babies are being born all the time. Why the fuss? What's so special about this child?

SAM: They believe the new star marks the importance of the child; and that He is the King of Kings.

HIGH PRIEST: But we already have a king! Herod the Great!

(JOSHUA *and* JACOB *grovel with ingratiating phrases, i.e., "No one could hope for a finer ruler," "He's the greatest," etc.)*

HIGH PRIEST: Enough of that! You don't have to go through the usual routine. He's not within earshot!

JOSHUA: There must be some mistake. If Herod's successor had just been born, surely he would know it.

SAM: Oh, this is useless! You guys don't know anything.

HIGH PRIEST: And who did you say you were, Sir?

SAM: Goldstein. Sam Goldstein . . . *Jerusalem Post.* I thought you people knew everything that went on. Don't you even have someone who does the prophecy bit?

JOSHUA: That only happens in Scripture, my boy. It went out with the Ark!

SAM: OK, forget it. This is getting me nowhere fast.

JACOB: Wait! My Lord, that lecture you gave last year—it had a prophecy.

HIGH PRIEST: What's he mumbling about?

JOSHUA: Which lecture?

JACOB: You know, about the prophecy of a future leader. It was in Deuteronomy, no . . . no . . . Isaiah . . . no, not Isaiah . . .

HIGH PRIEST: Well, go and find it, my boy!

(JACOB *goes to a very dusty rack of scrolls; gets steps to reach them; searches; dust flies everywhere; scrolls fall on the priests' heads.)*

JACOB: Here it is! *(Searches through the scroll.)*

HIGH PRIEST: This is ridiculous!

JACOB: No, listen. It was from the prophet, Micah:
>"But you, Bethlehem Ephrathah,
>though you are small among the
>   clans of Judah,
>out of you will come for me
>one who will be ruler over Israel."

JOSHUA: But that was written years ago.

JACOB: Yes, but it may indeed be the information they are seeking.

SAM: Well, OK, we'll give it a try. Thanks. *(Exits.)*

HIGH PRIEST: Pick these up, you bumbling oaf!

(Blackout.)

(SAM *and* RHONDA *speak in blackout.*)

SAM: Come on, RHON! We're going to Bethlehem!

RHONDA: Bethlehem? Why?

SAM: I don't know! Because the prophecy said so! I'm beginning to wonder if this whole thing isn't just a wild goose chase. We're gonna go all the way out to Bethlehem just to find that their "King of Kings" is just another babe like all the rest.

Scene 4: Shepherd's Village

(Villagers standing around a well.)

RHONDA: Sam, how much further?

SAM: To Bethlehem? I don't know. A couple of hours maybe.

RHONDA: I'm so thirsty. Can't we stop for a rest? There's a well over there in that village.

SAM: We've only been gone a few hours!

RHONDA *(pleading):* Sam!

SAM: OK, but hurry.

RHONDA: Quit griping! The kings have been traveling for several weeks. An extra half hour won't make much difference.

SAM: Half an hour! Look at that line for the well! You'd think they were having a clearance sale! What are they all yacking about. *(To women at the well)* Hey, girls! What's the big deal? People could die of thirst while you talk!

SYLVIA: Haven't you heard the news about the baby called "Jesus"?

SAM *(pushing forward):* Baby? What are you talking about?

RHONDA: Yes, tell us about the baby. Everything!

ETHEL: Well, it all started two nights ago . . .

BLANCHE *(interrupting):* Yeah, our husbands . . .

SYLVIA: They're shepherds . . .

ETHEL: Well, they were out on the hills . . .

SYLVIA: Watching over the flocks, ya' know . . .

ETHEL *(exasperated by all the interruptions):* I think they could figure that out, Sylvia? Will you let *me* tell them the story?

BLANCHE: An angel of the Lord appeared to them!

ETHEL: Pul-eeeease! *(Pulling herself together.)* An angel of the Lord appeared to them.

BLANCHE: I said that.

SYLVIA: She said that. *(Shoots them a look that could kill them both!)* Anyway, it was night, but the hillside was filled with bright, shining light.

BLANCHE: Yeah, Harvey said it scared 'em to death!

SYLVIA: But the angel told them not to be afraid, and that . . .

ETHEL *(cutting in):* . . . and that he had good news for everyone. He said that a Savior had been born in the city of David.

SAM: Hey, that's Bethlehem! That's just where we're headed!

SYLVIA: But that's not all that happened. Tell 'em about all the *other* angels, Ethel!

ETHEL: I was just getting to that part. Well, from out of nowhere came a whole bunch of other angels, praising God and saying,
> "Glory to God in the highest,
> and on earth peace, goodwill
> toward men."

BLANCHE: Then the angels told them they'd find a baby wrapped in swaddling cloths, and lying in a manger.

SYLVIA: In a stable.

SAM: A stable?! C'mon, woman, who are you trying to kid?

ETHEL: It's true. The baby was born to a young couple from Nazareth, who came to the city for the census.

RHONDA: But a *stable?*

SYLVIA: Yes. They arrived late, and there was nowhere else for them to stay. The innkeepers took pity on them.

STAN: Yeah . . . Reuben and Martha Dunn. They're good people.

SAM: It doesn't matter! Get on with the story! How do we find this stable?

STAN: You want to go to Bethlehem?

SAM *(sarcastically):* Well, we might as well, while we're in the neighborhood!

STAN: OK, I'll show you. I had to stay with the sheep that night, so I'm just about to go see the baby myself. But we need to hurry. It's getting dark already. Look, you can begin to see the lights of the city way over there!

RHONDA: Oh Sam, look! It's so pretty!

SAM: Come on, Wunderburgher! Don't go sentimental on me. We have a deadline to meet! (SAM, RHONDA, *and* STAN *exit as villagers gaze at Bethlehem in the distance.*)

(Blackout.)

Scene 5: Outside the Bethlehem Stable

(A group is standing in line to see the baby. SAM, RHONDA, *and* STAN *enter.)*

SAM: Well, we're here. Finally. Would ya' look at this crowd!

STAN: Yep, and there's the stable. Look! There's the star hanging over the place.

RHONDA: Would ya' look at this crowd! Do you think they've all come to see the baby?

STAN: Oh yes, miss. The shepherds in our village have been spreading the word to everyone. Well, I'll be saying "good-bye" now. Yo! Herb! *(Waves to someone in crowd.)*

RHONDA: I'm not about to wait in this line. Let's pull rank. Follow me. 'Scuse me. 'Scuse us please. Press! Press! Coming through!

MAN: Hey, watch who you're shoving, lady! *(To companion)* She must be one of those Women's Libbers.

SAM: We've been sent by King Herod. Let us pass.

(RHONDA *snaps pictures as they go to the front of the line. There are various negative reactions from the crowd.)*

RHONDA: Ahhhh, perfect timing, Sam. Looks like a group is just about to leave.

SAM: Yeah, but I don't want to go in yet. We've got to get some background info first. Phew! Is it hot right here, or is that just my imagination?

RHONDA: No, I feel it too. And I also feel sort of goose-bumpy. Hey, what's going on here?

MAN 1: It means that we are about to enter the presence of God, my friends. The Messiah . . . Emmanuel.

WOMAN 1: Go in and see for yourselves. Then you'll understand.

SAM: No, we need to interview a few in the crowd first. We'll catch the next group. Hey, you there! What brings you to this place?

MAN 2: I heard the news down at Marv's Feed Store. They're having a huge sale on sheep feed . . .

SAM: Uh, yes . . . moving right along. *(To* MAN 2) *Why* are you here?

MAN 2: To see if it's true.

RHONDA: To see if *what's* true?

WOMAN 2: Why, to see if this baby is really that *special.*

HERB: Zach says he saw angels the other night. He's telling everyone this child is the Son of God!

WOMAN 1: My sister was here yesterday, and she hasn't stopped talking about the little one.

WOMAN 2: The women down at the Discount Plaza told us to come at night, so we could see the star!

WOMAN 3: Personally, I think this story is highly exaggerated.

SAM: Do you really? How so?

WOMAN 3: Well, if you ask *me,* the shepherds who started this rumor probably were heavily tipping o' . . . well, you know.

RHONDA: Hmmmmmmm . . . a false rumor started by drunken shepherds, eh? *(To* SAM*)* Well, Herod would sure be pleased to hear that.

SAM: Yeah. Hey, Rhon . . . they're coming out. *(A group comes out; a new group goes in.)* Get a couple close-ups of their expressions. Man, they're in a daze.

(The THREE KINGS *are at the tail end of this outcoming group.* SAM *and* RHONDA *are taken completely by surprise.)*

SAM *(to* KINGS*)*: Hey! How'd you guys get here? You're supposed to be at *Herod's* palace!

BALTHAZAR: We followed the star of course. Did you think that after so many miles, it would fail us for the last short stretch?

MELCHIOR: When God starts you on something, He helps you right to the end.

GASPAR: Something like the birth of His son couldn't be left to chance. Go in and see for yourselves.

SAM: Well, the curiosity *is* killing me. I'm going in! *(Enters stable.)*

RHONDA: Hey! Wait for me! *(Snapping pictures, as she backs in.)*

(The CROWD *surrounds the* KINGS, *bombarding them with questions: "Is He the Son of God?" "How big is He?" "Did He cry?" "Did you get to hold Him?" [This question should be last and easily understood.])*

GASPAR: Yes, I held Him. And now that I've held Him in my arms, I feel such peace . . .

RHONDA *(reappearing with* SAM*)*: Sam, what's happened to me? Maybe you won't understand this, but something very personal happened to me in there. Somehow I feel that little Child is a part of me now. He has somehow changed my life!

SAM: I know. I feel it too, Rhon. I'm sure we'll understand it more completely when He becomes a man.

RHONDA: Oh, Sam! If Herod has his way, He'll never become a man! This baby Jesus could definitely threaten Herod's reign.

SAM: Rhonda, it's more than that. This Child could change *history!*

BALTHAZAR: Could? He will!

SAM: One thing for certain . . . He's not *just another child.*

RHONDA: But until everybody experiences what we're experiencing now, this Baby *will* be just another child born in Bethlehem . . .

SAM: Your Majesties, we must tell you something.

RHONDA: Herod has promised us a great deal of money for finding the Baby.

SAM: We know he plans to kill the Baby—and probably all baby boys in this area.

BALTHAZAR: Yes. It is just as I feared.

SAM: You mean you knew of his plot?

MELCHIOR: As we rested at the palace, all three of us were told of this in a dream.

SAM: Then please forgive us for being part of Herod's plot. We were so blinded by our own greed. But now that we've held Him, we believe we know who He is, and what He's come to do.

RHONDA: Sam, we must warn His parents that He's in danger.

BALTHAZAR: I assure you, my dear, you needn't fear that any harm will come to the Child. God is with them. He will protect them. Well, my friends, our long search is finally at an end. Now it's time to celebrate the coming of this tiny Child—with all mankind.

(Blackout.)